The Children's Book of
FIRST AID
SKILLS

Sophie Giles

Illustrated by Helen Stanton

AWARD PUBLICATIONS LIMITED

First aid is the help you can give to a person who is ill or injured (called a 'casualty'). The goal of first aid is to:

1. Keep the casualty alive

2. Stop them getting worse

3. Help them to recover

The first thing you must do is check for danger. Ask yourself: "Is it safe for me to help?" If you are not sure it is safe, you must call an adult or the emergency services instead.

! **Always check first to see if it's safe for you to help the casualty.**

Is it safe to help?

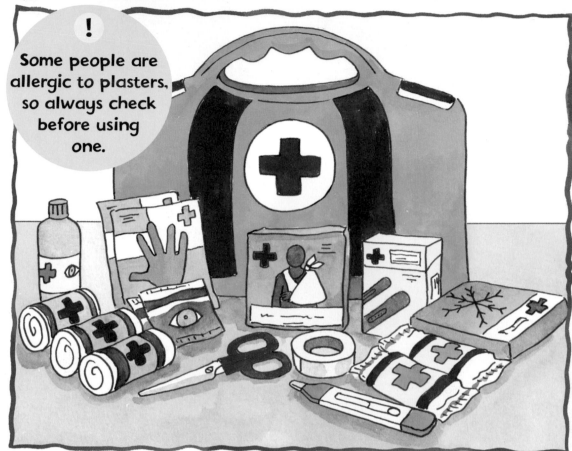

!

Some people are allergic to plasters, so always check before using one.

A first aid kit should contain all the things you need to deal with a minor injury. Make it a habit to check that the items are in date and any used equipment is replaced

as soon as possible. It should always be kept in the same place so you know where it is, and it can be found quickly. **Where is your first aid kit?**

! If the casualty is not breathing, call for help immediately.

1. Check for danger

2. Do they respond? *Are you OK?*

3. Is their airway clear?

4. Are they breathing?

5. Are they bleeding?

In an emergency, check in this order for:

Danger: Is it safe for you to help?

Response: Is the casualty responsive?

Airway: Is their airway open and clear?

Breathing: Are they breathing?

Circulation: Are they bleeding?

Danger
Response
Airway
Breathing
Circulation

 Remember: DR ABC

When someone has an asthma attack they find it difficult to breathe. This can happen during exercise or if a person has an allergic reaction to something such as

animal fur or dust. During an attack, Elsa's breathing becomes wheezy and noisy and she finds it hard to speak. **When can an attack happen?**

! Try to calm the casualty and slow down their breathing.

If Elsa starts to wheeze and gasp for air, she uses an inhaler. This relaxes the muscles in her chest and opens the airways, making it easier for her to breathe. As a first aider you can help to keep them calm.

! **Stay with the casualty until their breathing is normal again.**

Help to keep the person calm

Jacob is planning to surprise his dad by making him a cup of tea. But the kettle is heavier than he expects and he spills boiling water on his hand. The water scalds him badly. Jacob is in a lot of pain.

How is the kettle dangerous?

Dad helps Jacob to hold his hand under cold water for at least ten minutes to cool the scald and to reduce any damage. Next he loosely covers the hand with cling film and takes Jacob to hospital to be seen by a doctor.

! Hold under cold running water for 10 to 30 minutes.

Maddy bumped her nose at playtime and now she has a nosebleed. She sniffs and tips her head back to stop the bleeding, but a teacher quickly stops her. The blood  will run down her throat if she does that, causing her to be sick and making it difficult to breathe.

What should Maddy not do?

If a nosebleed lasts longer than 30 minutes, go to hospital.

Maddy's teacher helps her to sit down and tells her to pinch her nose, just above the nostrils, to slow the bleeding. Maddy breathes through her mouth, tips her head forwards and catches the blood with a tissue.

! Help the casualty to lean forward and pinch their nose.

Remember: always lean forwards

Ash has dropped a glass beaker and it has smashed. As he tries to clear it up he cuts his hand. His hand is bleeding badly, so he shouts his brother Joe for help. Ash feels dizzy and cold, and his skin is clammy. These are signs of shock.

How could Ash have avoided getting cut?

Joe checks the wound for any broken glass before pressing on it with a clean cloth. Because the bleeding is bad, he helps Ash to lie down, raising his legs. Joe covers Ash with a blanket to keep him warm and treat shock, and calls for help.

! **Check for debris, then apply pressure to the wound.**

Stem bleeding using pressure

Logan is out shopping with his best friend Vas. He begins to feel dizzy and starts to sweat. His skin has gone pale and cold. Suddenly, Logan faints. He falls to the floor and is unresponsive for a few moments.

What are two signs someone is feeling faint?

Vas has done first aid at school and knows to check Logan's airway, then raise his legs to help the blood flow back to his head. Soon Logan opens his eyes and is responsive again.

! **Raise their legs above their head.**

While playing in the garden, Anna sees a bird eat some berries on a bush. She decides to try one too, but the berries are poisonous. Soon she feels dizzy and has a

bad stomach ache. She goes into the house to tell her dad. **What should Anna have done if she wanted to eat the berries?**

!

Show the medical team what caused the poisoning – this helps them treat it more quickly.

Dad worries that Anna has been poisoned. He knows not to make her vomit. Because being poisoned is very serious and can kill, Dad takes her straight to hospital. Anna now knows not to eat wild berries unless she checks first with a grown up.

⚠️ **Do not make the casualty be sick.**

Call for help or get the casualty to a doctor

!
Talking while eating can be dangerous as it increases the risk of choking.

Mia and her mum are having dinner together, when suddenly Mum looks alarmed and starts to gasp for air. Mia realises that Mum is choking on a piece of food and encourages her to cough. But Mum cannot cough up the food and can't speak or breathe.

Why is Mia's mum choking?

First ask, "Are you choking?" If they are able to speak, they are just coughing.

Mia tells Mum to kneel down and lean forward. First she slaps her hard between the shoulder blades. When this doesn't work, Mia puts her arms around Mum's tummy, pulling inwards and upwards sharply and quickly, to help dislodge the food.

! Slap the casualty hard on the back five times.

Bend forward. Slap on their back 5 times

Kane and Molly love to play in the tree house in their garden. But one day, Kane slips and falls from the wooden ladder, and bangs his head on the ground.

Kane is crying. Molly runs to get Dad and tells him what has happened.

How could you try to protect your head in a fall?

Children have softer skulls than adults. Always treat any blow to the head with extra caution.

Molly holds a bag of frozen peas wrapped in a tea towel to Kane's head to reduce the swelling, while Dad gets a blanket to keep him warm. Dad says they must watch for signs of shock, and concussion: blurred vision, vomiting or extreme pain.

⚠ **If in doubt, seek medical assistance.**

Use an ice pack, and watch for concussion

Anya and her mum are playing in the garden, when Mum trips and falls awkwardly. Her wrist is swollen and painful. Unsure whether it's a break or sprain, Anya

knows to keep Mum's wrist as still as possible, so as not to do more damage.

Why does Anya keep Mum's wrist still?

! Keep the injured area supported and still, and use only ice and elevation until seen by a medical professional.

Anya supports Mum's wrist on a bunched-up coat, and uses an ice pack wrapped in a towel to reduce swelling. Then she tries to make Mum as comfortable as she can and calls her aunt to come and take Mum to see a doctor.

! **Support and raise the injured area if possible.**

Support the injury

Harry and Ryan are playing in the field when they disturb some wasps. They are both stung. But while Ryan's hand becomes red and sore, Harry's face swells and he struggles to breathe. He feels sick and is too weak to walk.

What has made Harry ill?

! Ice can help to reduce the swelling of minor stings.

Ryan knows Harry is allergic to wasp stings as he wears an allergy wristband. Ryan helps Harry use his auto-injector to stop the reaction to the sting. Then he helps Harry move away from the wasps, and calls for an ambulance.

! **Help the casualty to stay calm and to take their medication.**

Help them take their medication

Jess and her Uncle Arthur are having fun playing catch together in his garden, when Uncle Arthur stops suddenly. He clutches his chest and starts to gasp in pain. Jess notices that he is also short of breath.

What might be the cause of Uncle Arthur's chest pain?

Jess helps Uncle Arthur to sit down on the ground with his knees up, and loosens his collar and scarf to ease his breathing. Trying to keep him calm, she then calls an ambulance so that he can get medical help as soon as possible.

⚠️ **Call an ambulance as soon as possible.**

Loosen clothing and call for help

Glossary

Airway – the path air follows into and out of the body. In first aid, this usually refers to the nose, mouth and throat.

Allergic reaction – people with allergies can become sick or develop skin or breathing problems if they eat or come into contact with things that are usually harmless to other people. For example, particular foods – such as nuts, eggs or fish – or insect bites and stings. Severe allergic reactions can be dangerous, as the person may have difficulty breathing.

Casualty – someone who is sick or injured.

Danger – this could be anything that might injure you or others. It might have caused the accident, or it might just be something else nearby. Animals, electricity, fluids, gases, fast-flowing or deep water, and moving vehicles are examples of possible dangers.

Shock – shock is a medical emergency. It happens if a person's blood pressure falls suddenly, and the body's organs do not get enough blood – and oxygen – to function properly. Rapid heartbeat, irregular breathing and pale or clammy skin are all signs of shock.

Unresponsive – when a person does not react or respond to noise or contact – such as being spoken to, or gently shaken by the shoulders – they are unresponsive.

Recovery Position

If a casualty is unresponsive but breathing, you need to put them in the recovery position. This helps to keep the airway open so that the casualty can breathe easily and not choke while they are unconscious.

1. Kneel beside the casualty. Place the arm nearest to you at a right angle to the body.

2. Bring their other arm across their body, and gently twist their wrist so the back of their hand is against their cheek.

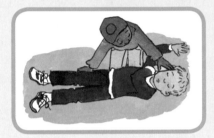

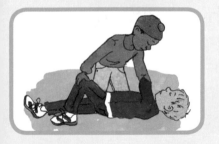

3. Reach across their body and lift the leg furthest away from you, so that their knee is bent and their foot is flat on the floor.

4. Keeping their hand against their cheek, use one hand to support the casualty's head, then gently pull their far knee towards you using your other hand. This will slowly roll the casualty onto their side.

5. Position the top leg so the casualty doesn't roll right onto their tummy. Holding the casualty's forehead and chin, tilt their head back slightly to open their airway.

Say hello, find out their name

"Hello! Can you hear me?"
"My name is [say your name]."
"What's your name?"

Reassure them, keep them calm

"Don't worry."
"I am going to get you some help."
"Just stay still and try to relax."

Find out information (from the casualty and any witnesses)

"When did it happen?"
"Where does it hurt?"
"How old are you?"
"Are you on any medication?"
LISTEN carefully to any answers.

Get help

Ask a friend or someone nearby
to go for help or to call an ambulance.

BEFORE calling the emergency services,
make sure you have all the CORRECT
information you need. This will help
save time, and maybe even a life!

Reassure them AGAIN

"Don't worry. "
"I will stay with you until help arrives."
"Stay still and try not to move."

Calling the Emergency Services

You may never have to call the emergency services, but in case you ever do, these simple steps are important to remember.

1. Call the emergency number. Write it here so you know it:

2. Ask for the ambulance service.

3. You will need to tell the call handler where to find you. If you do not know the address, look for landmarks, street names and road signs to describe where you are.

4. Explain what has happened and any symptoms or injuries the casualty has.

5. Follow the instructions given to you by the emergency services. Don't hang up until told to do so.

Know your home address and phone number

It is important to know your home address, in case you need the emergency services at home. You will also need to know your phone number, in case they need to call you back.

Write them in the boxes opposite.

In Case of Emergency (ICE)

ICE contacts and details of any medical conditions you have can be put into mobile phones, so the emergency services can access them even if your phone is locked.

First Aid Quiz

Now it's time to check what you have learned!

1. What does DR ABC – the five vital checks to make when first discovering a casualty– stand for?

A – Danger, Response, Airway, Breathing, Circulation

B – Danger, Rest, Ambulance, Bleeding, Call for help

C – Danger, Reponse, Aid, Breathing, Circulation

2. Which of these is a sign of shock?

A – clammy skin

B – white hair

C – chattering teeth

3. If you have a nosebleed you should:

A – tip your head backwards

B – tip your head forwards

C – tip your head to the side

4. What should you do when someone has chest pain?

A – Sit them down with their knees raised

B – Make them lie down flat

C – Keep them standing upright

5. What is the minimum time you should hold a burn or scald under cold running water?

A – 1 minute

B – 1 hour

C – 10 minutes

6. When someone has fainted you should:

A – raise their arms above their chest

B – stand them against the wall or other sturdy surface

C – raise their legs above their head

Answers: 1. A, 2. A, 3. B, 4. A, 5. C, 6. C

Encourage your child to use the stickers to help them remember what to do in first aid situations.

Loosen clothing and call for help

Raise their legs above their head

Danger
Response
Airway
Breathing
Circulation

Call for help or get the casualty to a doctor

Help to keep the person calm

Support the injury

Use an ice pack, and watch for concussion

Remember: always lean forwards

Help them take their medication

Bend forward. Slap on their back 5 times

Stem bleeding using pressure

Is it safe to help?

Hold scalds and burns under cold water

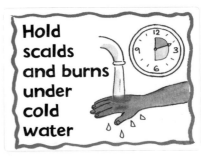